I want to thank my grandchildren, Alex and Garrett, for giving me the idea and Amy Clare, who kept me off the golf course and on target every day.

Amy

Matt

Alex

Copyright © 2003 by Carol Bassett

All rights reserved. No part of this book may be reproduced in any form or by any electronic or mechanical means, including information storage and retrieval systems, without permission in writing from the publisher.

First Edition

Printed in Hong Kong.

visit us at www.nubodconcepts.com

walk like a bear
stand like a tree
run like the wind

cool yoga, stretching and aerobic activities for cool kids
ages 6 - 12

written and designed by carol bassett
illustrated by amy clare

NUBOD
CONCEPTS

Introduction

OK, kids—are you ready to recharge your batteries, have some fun, and, at the same time, build strength, flexibility, and endurance?

Great! This book will show you some cool yoga and stretching exercises, plus some great outdoor sports you can do with a friend or alone. There is never a better time to learn about fitness than right now!! The younger you are, the better. Also, tell mom and dad that anybody can do these exercises. So why not have them join in the fun?

Whatever exercise you choose, it is better to do something everyday, than do nothing at all. The more you bring healthy activities into your life, the better you'll feel!

Get ready to have loads of fun and work those muscles, too!

A quick note on breathing:

Everyone knows how to breathe; but are you a chest breather? Chest breathers breathe in and out through their nose while only breathing into the top part of their chest. This is ok, but not when you're exercising! When exercising, you should inhale through your nose and exhale through your mouth; this supplies your body with more oxygen.

Table of Contents

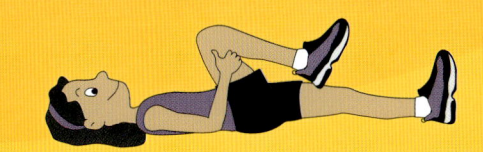

Stretches   6-11

Yoga   12-29
   Sun Salutation   28-29

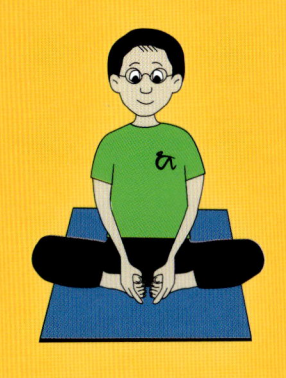

Aerobics   30-37

References   38

Workout Journal   39-40

Stretching

Before you start stretching, you need to know just how flexible you already are. Some people's bodies are naturally more flexible than others; remember, you're not competing against your friends or family to see who can stretch the furthest; you should only concentrate on your own body's flexibility.

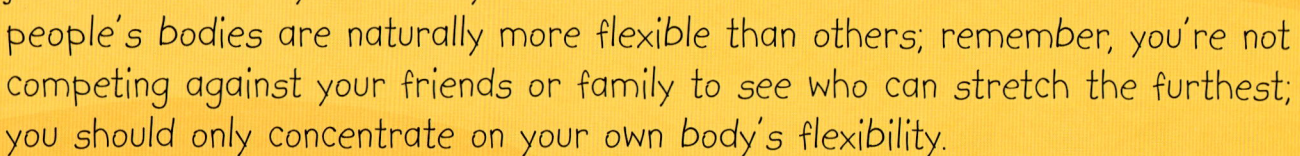

There is also a right way and wrong way to stretch. For instance, you should never bounce when you're stretching because you could over-stretch. Stretching should feel good when done correctly. Most importantly, make stretching a regular part of your day. Each time you stretch, you will become more flexible. Remember to breath!

Bounce up, Buddy Remember bouncing is for trampolines, not stretching.

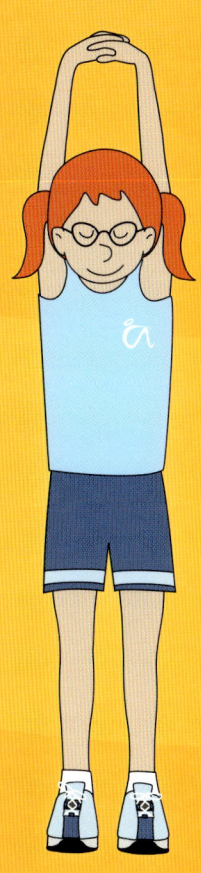

Stand tall, and wiggle a little; wiggling will help you stand even taller; interlace your fingers above your head, and, with your palms facing upward, push your arms slightly back and up. You'll feel the stretch in your arms, shoulders, and upper back. Hold to the count of 10, breathing in through your nose and out through your mouth.

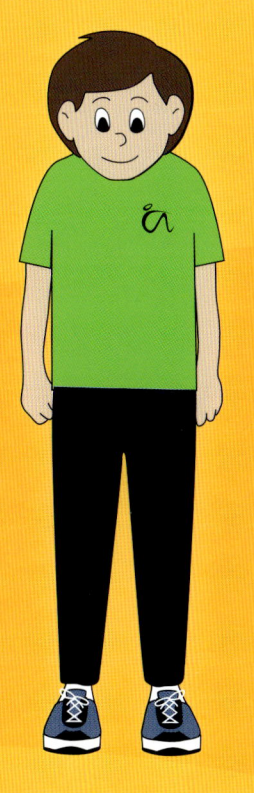

Very slowly raise your shoulders toward your ears. Hold and count to 5; then lower your right ear to your right shoulder. Hold to the count of 5, and then repeat on the left side; do this 5 times; also, try rolling your shoulders forward 5 times and back 5 times. This will help loosen your neck and shoulders.

Standing tall like a tree, try flexing your knees slightly. Take hold of your left elbow with your right hand, and slowly bend to the right. Hold to the count of 10 and repeat on the left side, holding your right elbow with your left hand. Remember breathe in through your nose and out through your mouth.

Interlace your fingers behind your back; slowly turn your elbows inward while keeping your arms straight. You'll feel this stretch in your shoulders, arms, and chest. Hold for the count of 10. When you're ready, very slowly try raising your arms up behind you. If you want, try a more challenging stretch; bend over and just hang for the count of ten; of course, you're breathing all the time.

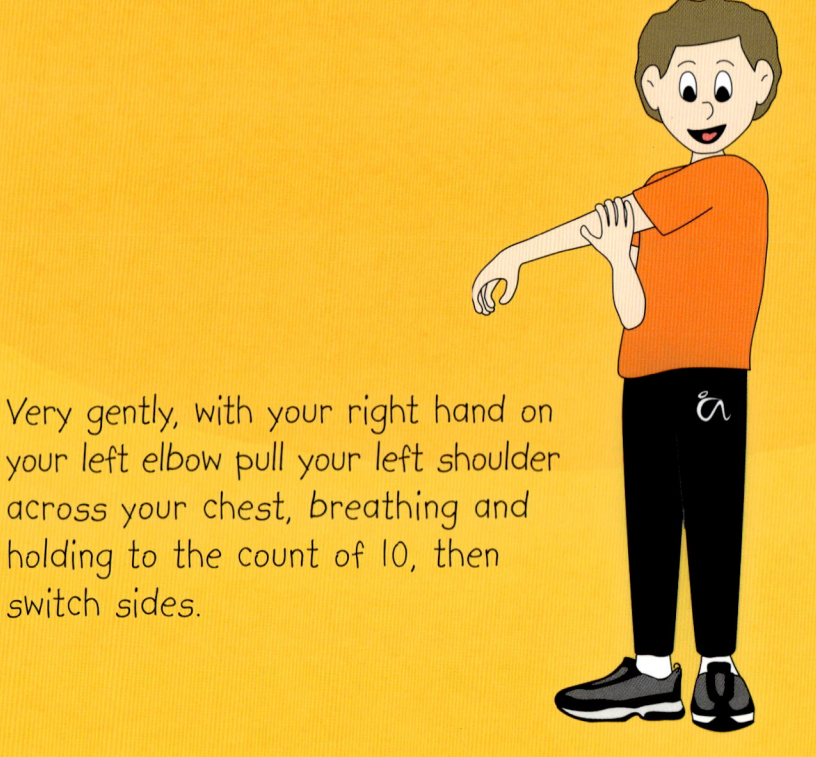

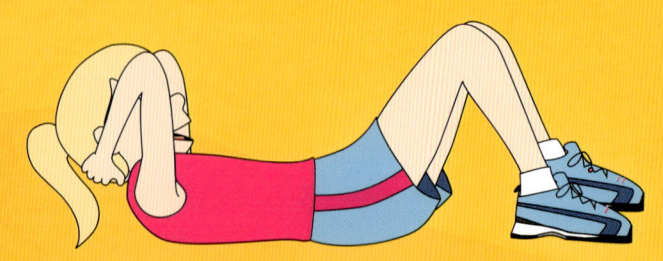

Very gently, with your right hand on your left elbow pull your left shoulder across your chest, breathing and holding to the count of 10, then switch sides.

This exercise stretches your upper spine and neck. While lying on the floor, interlace your fingers behind your head. Now slowly pull your head forward, without straining your neck, until you feel a small stretch in the back of your neck. Hold for the count of 10. Repeat 3 more times. This exercise should be done very gently.

To stretch your calf, standing one to two feet from a solid support, such as a wall; slowly lean forward; rest your head on your forearms; bend your left leg and keep your right leg straight behind you. Now slowly lean forward, keeping your back flat; hold and count to 10; now switch sides.

Lay down on your back. Put your hands under your right knee, and pull your right leg into your chest. Hold to the count of 10. Now you can switch to the other leg. Now bring both legs into your chest, and rest there to the count of 10. This stretch is good for the back of your legs and hips.

You can do this next stretch standing or lying on your stomach. Take hold of your left foot with your right hand. Very gently pull your heel towards your bottom. Hold and count to 10; then change legs. You should feel this stretch in your thighs.

Move one leg forward until your knee of the forward leg is directly over your ankle. Your other leg is resting on the floor, don't bounce Now count to 10, feel the stretch, then switch sides.

side view

Sitting up tall put the soles of your feet together holding your toes with your hands. Very gently lean forward, bending at your hips, pulling yourself towards your feet. This will stretch your inner thighs. Hold this position and slowly count to 10. Repeat 3 times.

Sitting with your right leg straight, bend your left leg and cross it over your right leg. Place your left foot on the ground. Now place your right hand on the floor behind you, and then turn your shoulder towards your left side. You'll feel this stretch in your lower back and the side of your hip. Now change sides, remembering to breathe.

side view

Lie on your back and raise your right leg toward the sky with your foot flat. When starting this stretch, use a towel around the bottom of your foot. Hold the ends of the towel, keeping your back flat on the floor, and slowly count to 10; then repeat with the other leg.

Yoga

Yoga is terrific because you need very little space to do it, nor do you need expensive workout attire; all you need is loose fitting clothing, and no shoes! If you're not exercising on a carpet, however, you will need a yoga mat.

Yoga makes your body feel good both inside and out. The physical benefits include building your strength and flexibility, and lengthening and strengthening your spine.

Furthermore, yoga allows positive power into your body and rejuvenates your energy centers. Every person has energy centers, which are called Chakras (see the next page for a detailed description). Yoga keeps these energy centers balanced, which can lead to good mental and spiritual health.

Chakras (shah-krah-z)

Chakras are energy centers in the body. They are located from the top of your head to the base of your spine.

Here is a general guide to what the chakras represent:

1. The first chakra is located at the base of the spine and represents our instincts. It's the color red.

2. The second chakra, the stomach, represents our creation. It's the color orange.

3. The third chakra, the navel or belly button, represents what we eat, drink and digest. It's the color yellow.

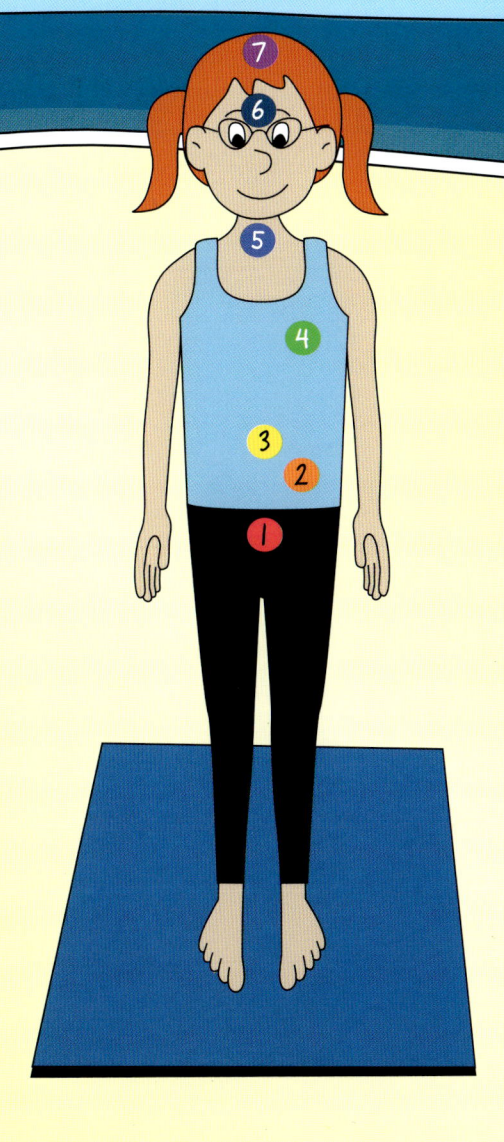

4. The fourth chakra, the heart, represents love, kindness and understanding. It's the color green.

5. The fifth chakra, the throat, represents communication. It's the color blue.

6. The sixth chakra, the forehead, represents insight and awareness. It's the color sapphire.

7. The seventh chakra, at the top of the head, is the center for all spiritual enlightenment. It's associated with the color violet.

Mountain Pose

The mountain pose is one of the main Yoga exercises. It teaches you correct posture, and strengthens your back; it also helps focus your mind.

- Stand with your feet parallel, at least 6-8 inches apart. Keeping your hands at your sides, focus on a point in front of you, and try to stand still.

- In your mind, pretend that you're a mountain. Think how strong and stable it makes you feel. There is nothing stronger than this mountain.

- Stay in this position for 10-15 seconds.

Flamingo Pose

This pose strengthens your balance, stretches your quadriceps, and improves your posture. Did you know that a flamingo stands on one leg?

- Focus on a point in front of you. This will help you balance.
- When you're ready, raise one leg, bending it at the knee. Be sure to raise your foot slowly so you don't lose your balance.
- Grab hold of your foot with your hand, making sure it's the hand on the same side as your foot.
- Now raise your other hand to the sky.
- **Try holding 5-10 counts on each foot.** Don't get discouraged if you can't hold the pose without losing your balance. It just takes practice.

Tree Pose

The tree pose improves your balance and strengthens your back and legs. If you're having trouble standing on one foot, hold on to a chair or lean up against a wall.

- Begin by standing with your feet parallel, and your arms at your sides.. Focus on a point in front of you.

- Imagine you are a tree and you have roots growing from your toes that are keeping you attached to the ground. Try and stand as tall as an oak.

- Slowly bring up one foot and place it on the inside of your standing leg anywhere between your ankle and your knee.

- Now try putting your hands together in front of you. When you're able to balance, lift your hands above your head. Now you look like a tree!

- Breathe and hold as long as you feel comfortable then repeat with your other leg.

Downward Dog Pose

This pose imitates a dog stretching. It gives you a great stretch and strengthens your back, arm, and leg muscles. It will pep up your mind as the blood flows to your head.

- Drop down onto your knees and hands. Spread your fingers and press them into the floor. Push onto your toes and slowly begin to raise your knees off the floor, stretching your bottom upward towards the sky.

- Straighten the back of your legs if you can, or keep them bent. You will feel the stretch in the back of your legs.

- Relax your neck and let your head dangle.

- Hold this pose to the count of 10.

Bear Walk Pose

The bear pose will loosen you up; have some fun, and take some weight off your feet! This pose will strengthen your arms, wrists, legs, and ankles.

- You'll begin with the downward dog pose (page 17)
- Step forward with your left arm and right leg, and then with your right arm and left leg.
- Keep walking with your arms and legs, keeping them straight, if you can. Pretend you're a bear looking for food in the forest.
- Try walking all around the room.

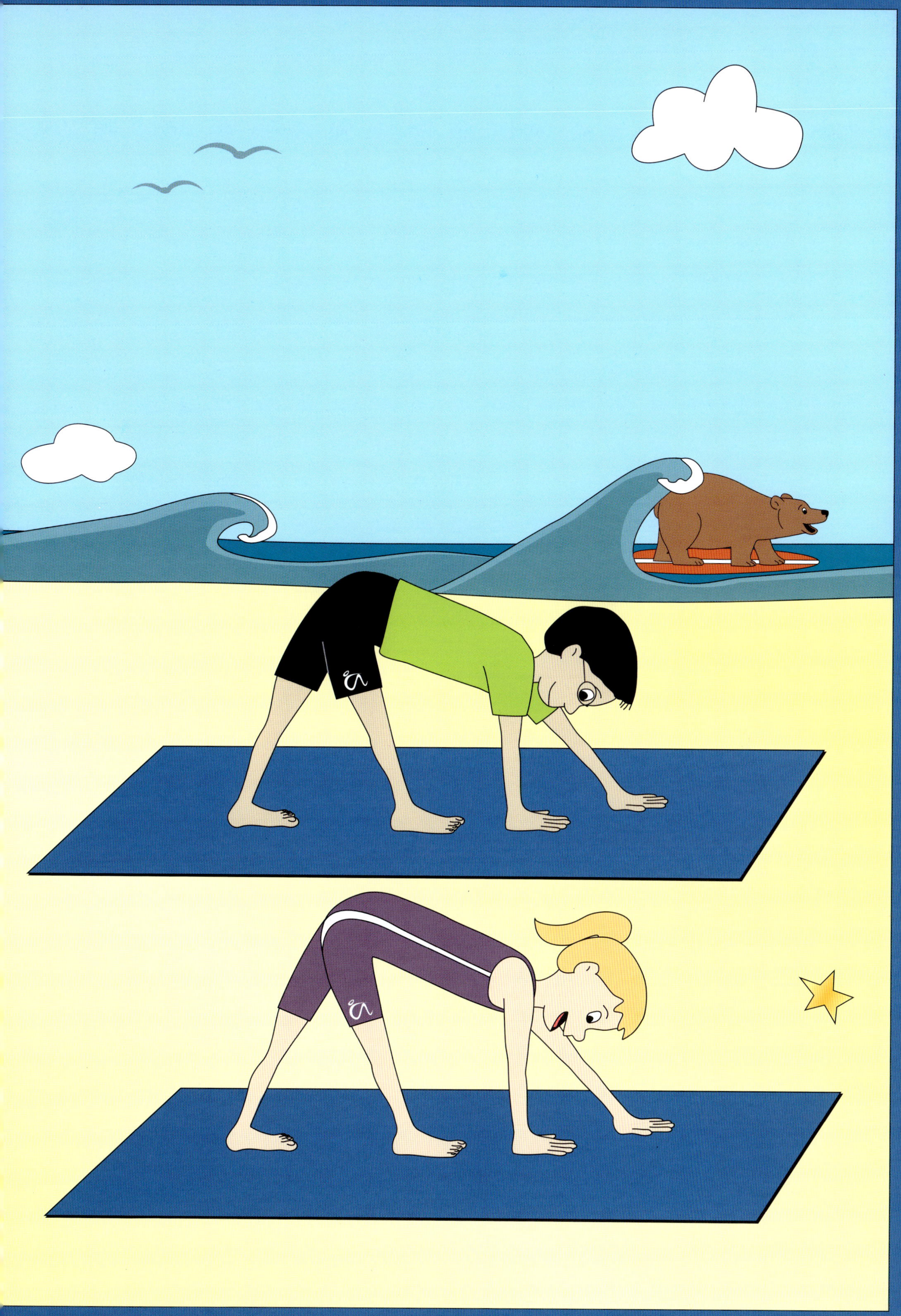

Rainbow Pose

The rainbow pose can be a little hard, but it's terrific! You're opening the rib cage and making your arms, legs, and body stronger. At the same time, it improves your balance and focus.

- Begin with the downward dog pose (page 17). Your entire body forms an upside down V.

- Slowly turn your whole body to the left, dropping your hips so your body forms a slanting line from your head to your feet. Your right leg rests on your left leg, and your feet should be stacked on top of each other. This takes lots of strength from your whole body, so go slowly.

- Bring your right arm and rest it on your right hip so that you're balancing on your left arm and left leg.

- When you feel comfortable in the pose, raise your right arm to the sky.

- Count to 10, then slowly roll back into a downward dog pose, and repeat on the other side.

Butterfly Pose

This pose is fun, and it really strengthens your hips. Remember, that some people are naturally more flexible than others!

- Sitting on the floor, place the soles of your feet together. Your legs will be in a diamond shape.
- Hold your feet together with your hands; now **slowly** make your knees go up and down like a butterfly.
- Raise your knees slowly up and down 10 times.
- Keep your torso tall and be sure to breathe.
- Now picture yourself taking off from a tree branch, flying over all your favorite places.

Boat Pose

In the boat pose your body is the boat and your arms are the oars. This pose increases your balance and concentration while strengthening your stomach and leg muscles. It will also help calm your mind.

- Sit with your legs bent and the soles of your feet on the floor.

- Keeping your hands on the floor, very slowly lean backwards and lift your feet off the floor, until your legs and body are balanced. Now straighten your legs as much as you can.

- Put your arms out in front of you. They should be parallel to the floor; then FOCUS on a point in the room (this will help you stay balanced).

- For more fun, make-believe you're floating in a lake. Ask Mom or a friend to join you to be his or her own boat. Be sure to feel the warm sun, see the blue sky, feel the gentle breeze, and don't forget to listen to the waves!

- Try and hold to the count of 5. Do this twice.

start like this →

Bridge Pose

The bridge pose forms a bridge using just your body. It increases flexibility in your spine and builds strength in your thighs and bottom, while, at the same time, opening up your chest.

- Lie down on your back and bend your knees with your feet on the floor. Place your feet hip-distance apart and your arms at your sides.
- In your mind, pretend there is a rope attached to your belly button pulling it up toward the sky.
- Imagine it's lifting your stomach, hips and thighs until they cannot raise any further. Keep pressing your feet and hands into the floor.
- Hold the bridge up to the count of 10. Repeat 3 times.

Snake Pose

The snake pose keeps your spine, shoulders, elbows and wrists flexible.

- Lie on your stomach with your legs as straight and as close together as possible.

- Place your forehead on a mat, and put your hands face down on the floor with your elbows next to your chest.

- As you inhale, slowly lift your head and neck; this will make a small arch in your upper spine.

- Now lift your hands off the mat, and keep them close to your chest. Count to 30, then release.

- Repeat 3 or 4 times.

- While counting, why don't you hiss like a snake!

Shark Pose

This pose takes some strength. It also improves flexibility in your spine and neck. You'll use your arms, stretch your shoulders, and open your chest.

- Lie on your stomach and bend your knees so your feet point up toward the ceiling.
- Bring both arms behind your back and interlock your fingers.
- Now straighten your arms behind you by lifting your hands. Go as high as you can, stretching your arms and hands as if they were a great white shark's fin.
- Now raise your upper body leading with your head, and hold for 10 seconds. This feels so good, and is one of my favorite exercises.
- For some fun, wiggle like a shark in the water.
- Repeat 3 times.

Mouse Pose

Try spending some time by yourself each morning or each evening, just before bedtime, because this pose is very relaxing.

- Sit on your knees, then, keeping your arms at your sides, sit back on your heels. Keep your toes flat, without curling them under.
- Slowly bend forward until your forehead rests on the floor. You can use a pillow, if you like.
- Keeping your arms at your sides, close your eyes and relax your face.
- Allow yourself to chill out for 1 minute.

Meditation Pose

Meditation can be done lying down or sitting up. You just need to keep your mind still.

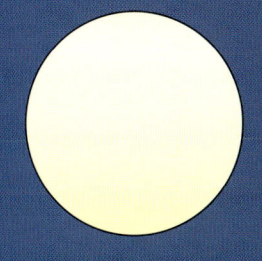

- If you choose to sit, start by crossing your legs and resting your hands on your knees.

- Pay close attention to your breathing. Feel your breath moving in and out of your body. You can even hear yourself breathe, if you listen closely.

- Think of your very favorite color. Take a deep breath and think of that color surrounding you. Now imagine a big white cloud. See yourself climbing onto the cloud and lying down. You should feel very calm.

- Keeping very still, pretend that you and the cloud are traveling to a make-believe place. Remember to keep breathing very slowly.

- Start by doing this 5 minutes, and work up to 15 minutes.

- Do this every day to feel the most relaxed.

your hands should look like this

Sun Salutation

1. Stand tall in the mountain pose which you you saw on page 14.

2. Exhale and bring your palms together in the prayer position in front of your heart.

13. Cross your thumbs then reach them out, up overhead and slightly behind you creating a gentle arch in your back.

14. Return to the mountain pose with your hands back in the prayer position.

Repeat the cycle lunging with your left leg first.

12. Inhale and step your left leg back so you're in a lunge. Stay close to the ground. Roll up to a standing position.

11. Exhale, step your left then right foot forward and return to the forward bending position.

10. Exhale, curl your toes under and raise your hips back into downward facing dog. Hang your head, feel your back leg muscles coming alive.

3. Inhale and slowly raise your arms over your head (interlace your fingers and cross your thumbs).

4. Look up toward your hands and carefully bend backward creating a gentle arch in your back.

5. Exhale slowly. Lower your arms and upper body in one motion to the floor. Bend your knees to protect your back.

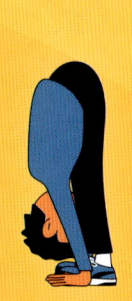

Just doing the sun salutation 2 times around every day can make your body feel better. Remember to breathe.

6. Inhale and step back with your right leg so you're in a lunge. Stay close to the ground.

7. Inhale and step your left leg back raising your hips in the downward facing dog pose (page 17). You'll look like an upside down V.

8. Exhale as you lower your knees, chest and chin to the ground. Relax your feet and point your toes backwards. Slide forward into the snake pose (page 24).

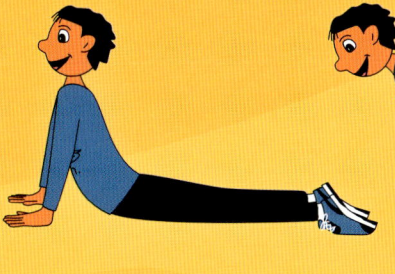

9. Inhale and raise your body off the mat, slowly arching your back. Keep your head back and hands pressed into the mat. You now look like a king cobra.

Aerobics

You want to start any type of aerobic exercise with a warm-up of 2-5 minutes; try stretching, jumping jacks or fast walking.

Now you're ready to spend at least 15-30 minutes cycling, swimming, running, playing soccer, or shooting hoops. You just need to keep moving at a pace that feels good for you. Listen to your body. It will tell you if you are pushing too hard or not hard enough.

Then, finally, you'll cool down another 5 minutes, stretching out your calves, thighs, and lower and upper back.

Does this sound like work? It doesn't have to be; it can be fun. If you think about building a stronger body, healthier lungs and heart, it's all worth it. This also will help you concentrate better in school.

Don't leave mom and dad out! They can do this right along beside you.

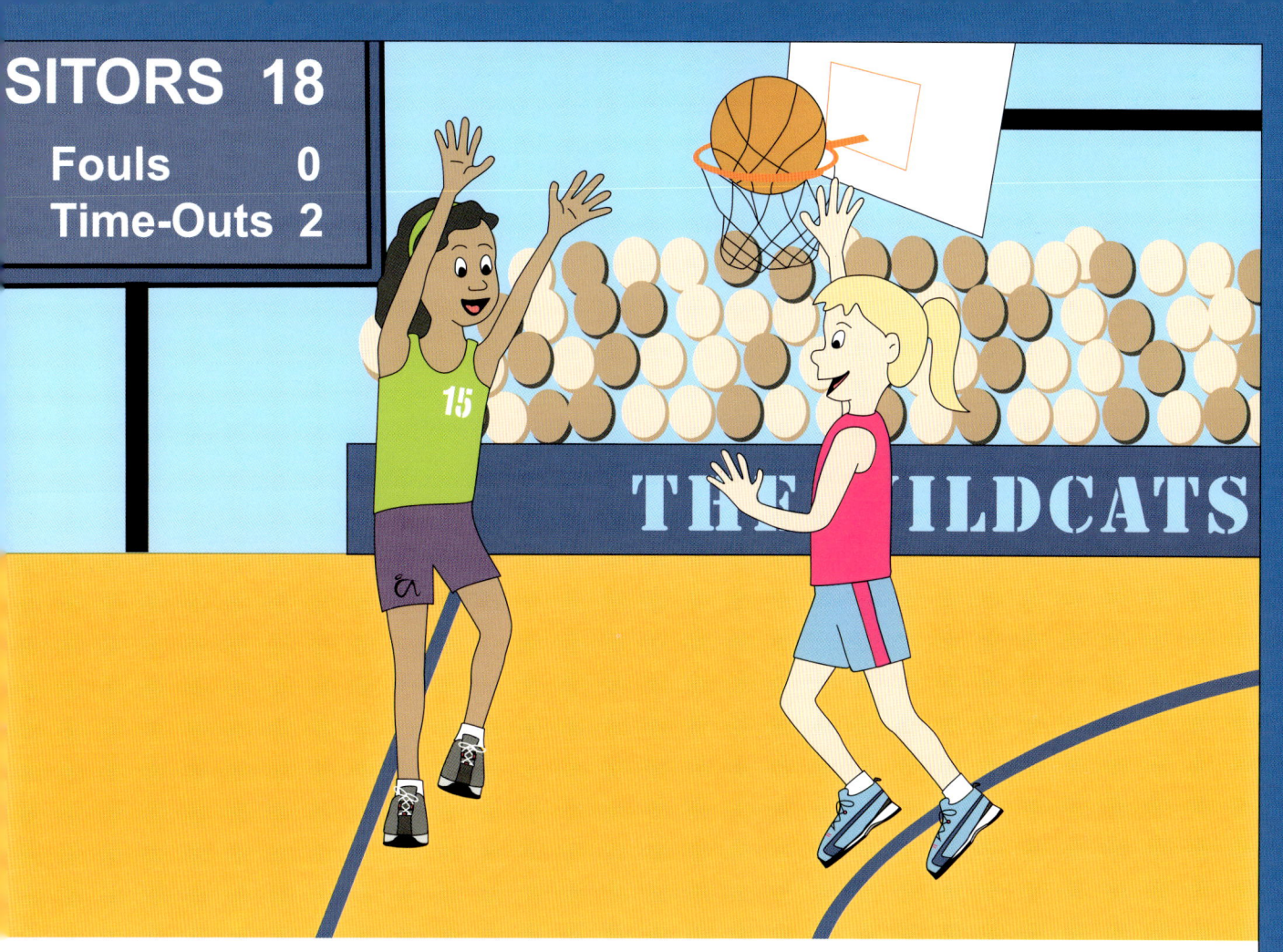

Basketball

Basketball is the most popular participant sport in the United States. You find basketball courts at school playgrounds, school gyms, backyards, and parks. It takes only one person to shoot baskets, or you can find a friend, and just play against each other. All you need is a ball and a basket.

When playing basketball you develop muscle power, balance, flexibility, eye-hand coordination, plus you become faster on your feet.

Try these stretches before you shoot hoops.

Bicycling

Riding your bike is a great way to get exercise; not only are you outside in the fresh air, but you can also be with your friends.

Having a bike that is the right size for your height and weight is very important. Equally important is a good helmet. Make sure it fits correctly: not too tight or too loose.

Even your arms need a good stretch before pedaling around town.

Jumping Jacks

This is my very favorite exercise. You can do these anywhere. Start with your hands at your sides and your legs together. Now jump and bring your hands straight over your head and land with your feet wide apart.

Jump again and bring your hands back to your sides with your feet close together. Try it now. Try it in front of a mirror to see if you look like the picture.

Stretch before you leap.

BIRDIE, BIRDIE IN THE SKY,
WHY'D YOU DO THAT IN MY EYE?
BIRDIE, BIRDIE IN THE SKY,
GEE, I'M GLAD THAT COWS DON'T FLY.

Jumping Rope

Jumping rope requires very little space, and it takes less time to get the aerobic exercise you need. It not only exercises the whole body, but also stimulates your mind. It sharpens your reactions and improves your coordination as well. You can jump rope alone or with a friend.

A good pair of athletic shoes that supports your ankles and cushions the balls of your feet is important when jumping rope, but NEVER jump rope barefoot.

These stretches will warm up your jumping muscles.

Running

Our ancient ancestors had to walk and run to survive. Of course, we don't have a Saber Tooth Tiger chasing after us today! Now we can enjoy running and notice how good it makes us feel by building our heart and lungs. When you start running, go slowly and work up to longer distances. Soon you'll run like the wind!

Ask your mom or dad to run a race with you, or race with some of your friends.

A good stretch before running can help avoid pulled muscles.

Soccer

Soccer is a game of physical and mental challenges. It builds your aerobic endurance, your flexibility, and your strength in the lower half of your body. During just one game, players may run several miles.

Even though soccer is a team sport, you can practice soccer with a friend or by yourself. If you have a soccer ball and a yard with enough space to dribble back and forth, you can develop the timing needed to pass the ball to a teammate.

Soccer uses lots of different muscles so be sure to warm them up.

Swimming

Swimming is a healthy way to exercise. You get your workout by moving your arms and legs against the resistance of the water.

Swimming has lots of advantages over other aerobic exercises. It is less stressful to the joints in your body, and the muscles on both sides of your body get an equal workout.

Everyone can benefit from swimming. You're never too young, or too old to start. If you happen to have asthma or other breathing problems, swimming is the very best way to exercise. Just remember: if you can float, you can swim.

Stretching can help you pull and kick harder.

References

The following books were consulted, and found useful, during the research for this book.

Jodi B. Komitor, M.A., and Eve Adamson. The Complete Idiot's Guide to Yoga with Kids, Indianapolis, IN Alpha Books, 2000.

Stella Weller. Yoga for Children, Thorsons 1996.

Bob Anderson. Stretching. Bolinas, CA, Shelter Publications, Inc. 2000.

Glen Vecchione. The Jump Rope Book, New York, N.Y. Sterling Publishing Company, Inc. 1995.

Kenneth H. Cooper M.D. Fit Kids! Nashville, TN, Broadman & Holman Publishers. 1999.

Joseph A. Luxbacher. Soccer – Steps to Success, Champaign, IL Human Kinetics Publishers, Inc. 1996.

David G. Thomas. Swimming – Steps to Success, Champaign, IL Human Kinetics Publishers, Inc. 1996.

Woof oof woofoof! (same time tomorrow!)

Workout Journal

How many stars can you earn each week? If you exercise 10 minutes a day, you get one star. Try to earn three or four stars a day. You can accomplish this easily by doing a couple yoga poses, a few stretches, some jumping

	Yoga	Stretching	Aerobics
Sunday			
Monday			
Tuesday			
Wednesday			
Thursday			
Friday			
Saturday			
Sunday			
Monday			
Tuesday			
Wednesday			
Thursday			
Friday			
Saturday			
Sunday			
Monday			
Tuesday			
Wednesday			
Thursday			
Friday			
Saturday			

Cut this page out and keep it nearby when you exercise.

Workout Journal

jacks, or you can run around the block a couple of times, and get some fresh air as a bonus. The time will fly by; you'll have lots of fun, and, in no time, you'll have these pages filled with stars.

	Yoga	Stretching	Aerobics
Sunday			
Monday			
Tuesday			
Wednesday			
Thursday			
Friday			
Saturday			
Sunday			
Monday			
Tuesday			
Wednesday			
Thursday			
Friday			
Saturday			
Sunday			
Monday			
Tuesday			
Wednesday			
Thursday			
Friday			
Saturday			

Cut this page out and keep it nearby when you exercise.